GREAT 20TH CENTURY EXPEDITIONS

ARMSTRONG LANDS ON THE MOON

Gordon Charleston

Dillon Press
New York

First American publication 1994 by Dillon Press, Macmillan Publishing Company, 866 Third Avenue, New York, NY 10022

Macmillan Publishing Company is part of the Maxwell Communication Group of Companies.

First published in Great Britain in 1994 by Zoë Books Limited

A ZOË BOOK

Devised and produced by
Zoë Books Limited
15 Worthy Lane
Winchester
Hampshire SO23 7AB
England

Printed in Italy by Grafedit SpA
Design: Jan Sterling, Sterling Associates
Picture research: Faith Perkins
Illustrations and maps: Gecko Limited
Production: Grahame Griffiths

10 9 8 7 6 5 4 3 2 1

Library of Congress Cataloging-in-Publication Data

Charleston, Gordon.
    Armstrong lands on the moon / Gordon Charleston
      p. cm. — (Great 20th century expeditions)
    ISBN 0-87518-530-4
    1. Project Apollo (U.S.)—Juvenile literature.
    2. Space flight to the moon—Juvenile literature.
    3. Armstrong, Neil, 1930- —Juvenile literature.
    [1. Project Apollo (U.S.) 2. Space flight to the moon 3. Armstrong, Neil, 1930- .] I. Title.
    II. Series.
    TL789.8.U6A5247 1994
    629.45'4'0973—dc20   93-32918

Summary: Describes the famous moon landing, and the events leading up to it, by U.S. astronauts in 1969.

Photographic acknowledgments

The publishers wish to acknowledge, with thanks, the following photographic sources:

NASA (National Aeronautics and Space Administration): 4, 5t & b, 6t & b, 9t, 11, 12, 13, 15bl & br, 16t, 17, 18, 19, 20, 21, 22, 23t, 26, 27l & r, 28t & b, 29t & b; The Science Photograph Library: title (NASA), 8 (Novosti), 9b (Novosti), 10 (Novosti), 16b (NASA), 23b (NASA), 25t & b (NASA)

Cover photographs courtesy of NASA

The publishers have made every effort to trace the copyright holders, but if they have inadvertently overlooked any, they will be pleased to make the necessary arrangement at the first opportunity.

Contents

"One giant leap for mankind"

At 10:56 P.M. on July 20, 1969, Neil Armstrong, an American **astronaut**, climbed out of a **spacecraft** called *Eagle*. He moved slowly down a ladder. As he stepped off the ladder onto the gray powder of the moon's surface, he spoke to millions of people watching on television on earth. He said, "That's one small step for a man, one giant leap for mankind."

Armstrong and his fellow astronaut, Edwin "Buzz" Aldrin, had become the first people to land on the moon.

Five days earlier, Armstrong, Aldrin, and another astronaut, Michael Collins, had blasted off from the **launchpad** on earth. They had traveled 240,000 miles (385,000 km) through space.

The orbiting moon

The moon is the earth's nearest companion in space. It can easily be seen in the night

▲ The earth seen from the moon

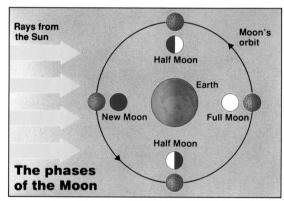

The phases of the Moon

Rays from the Sun

Moon's orbit

Half Moon

Earth

New Moon

Full Moon

Half Moon

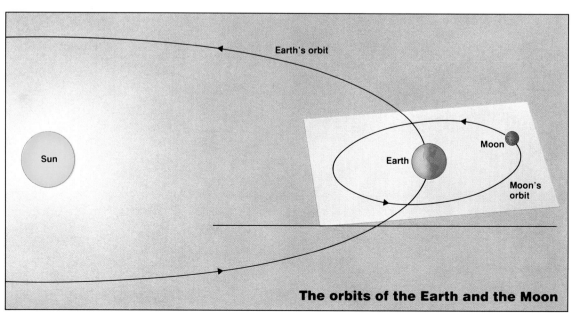

Earth's orbit

Sun

Earth

Moon

Moon's orbit

The orbits of the Earth and the Moon

▲ As a spacecraft leaves the earth to go into space, the astronauts inside no longer feel the pull of the earth's gravity. They become weightless and can float around inside the spacecraft.

sky when there are no clouds. The moon is 80 times smaller than the earth. The moon is called the earth's **satellite** and goes around, or circles, the earth in a path called an **orbit**. The moon takes about a month to orbit the **planet** earth.

At certain times, as the moon moves around the earth, the earth comes between the sun and the moon. It blocks light from the moon, so that the moon looks different in shape as sunlight falls on some, or none, of its surface. Only at "full" moon do we see the whole of one side of the moon in light. People used the different appearance of the moon in the night sky to measure time. They set up a calendar based on "moonths," or months.

Gravity

When you throw a ball up into the sky, it falls back to the ground. The force that "pulls" the ball back is known as **gravity**.

The earth and the moon are held together in space by gravity. They "pull" each other. The moon is lighter than the earth, so it cannot escape from the earth's pull—it is trapped in the earth's orbit.

People weigh less on the moon than they do on earth, because the moon's gravity is weaker than earth's. An astronaut wearing a **space suit** might weigh about 350 pounds (160 kg) on earth, but on the moon that weight would be only about 60 pounds (28 kg).

The moon does have some pull on the earth. It affects the movement of the seas on earth. High and low tides are caused by the position of the moon. Each day there are high tides when the moon is nearest and its pull is strongest. When the moon's pull is weakest, the tide is low.

▼ A spacecraft in orbit above the earth

Into space

▲ *Explorer 1*

Rockets were invented by Chinese people about two thousand years ago, but it was not until about 100 years ago that Western scientists and engineers began to study rocket power. In the 1890s, a Russian teacher, Konstantin Tsiolkovsky, worked on the idea that rocket power might be strong enough to lift a spacecraft, but he did not build any rockets. In 1926, an American, Robert Goddard, was the first person to launch a rocket.

The first rockets were developed for use in World War II. After the end of the war, in the 1940s, scientists began to think about rockets as part of space exploration. A team led by the German scientist Wernher von Braun developed more powerful rockets. They aimed to produce a rocket that would have enough power to send a spacecraft out beyond the pull of the earth's gravity. To do this, a rocket would need a speed of more than 26,000 mph (42,000 kph).

▼ The launch of *Explorer 1*

Sputnik 1 and *2*

On October 4 1957, Russian scientists successfully launched the world's first satellite, *Sputnik 1*, into space. Inside was a battery-powered radio transmitter that sent out a "bleep, bleep" signal. *Sputnik 1* was shaped like a ball, measured 23 inches (58 cm) across, and weighed 183 pounds (83 kg). One month later, *Sputnik 2* was launched. The space age had begun.

Explorer 1

In the United States, the National Aeronautics and Space Administration (NASA) was set up to coordinate and develop space exploration. On January 31, 1958, the Americans launched their first satellite, *Explorer 1*. It went into orbit higher than either of the two *Sputniks*, and it weighed only 10.5 pounds (4.75 kg).

Atmosphere

The planet earth is surrounded by a layer of gases that is called the **atmosphere**. These gases include **oxygen** and carbon dioxide, and make up the air that human beings need to breathe to stay alive. Gravity holds the atmosphere in place around the earth. The air in the atmosphere presses down on the earth and is called **air pressure**. The higher you go away from the earth's surface, the lighter the air becomes. Beyond the earth's atmosphere, there is no air and no air pressure. Everything is weightless, and humans cannot breathe.

Reentering the earth's atmosphere

A spacecraft must reenter the earth's atmosphere at exactly the right speed and direction, or angle. If it comes in too fast or its angle of entry is too steep, it could be set on fire. This is because heat is created by the air pressure in the atmosphere. If the angle is too narrow, the spacecraft might "bounce" on top of the layer of atmosphere. If it does this, it will be lost in space.

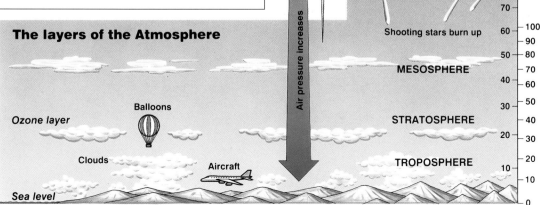

Temperature increases

miles   km

Safellites

— 500

300 —

— 400

200 —

THERMOSPHERE — 300

— 200

Air pressure increases

Shooting stars burn up   60 — 100
                                — 90
                          50 — 80
            MESOSPHERE   — 70
                          40 — 60
                                — 50
                          30
            STRATOSPHERE   — 40
                          20 — 30

100 —
90 —
80 —
70 —

The layers of the Atmosphere

Ozone layer

Balloons

Clouds

Aircraft   TROPOSPHERE   — 20
                          10 — 10

Sea level   — 0

The first astronauts

The successes with *Sputnik* and *Explorer* had shown that spacecraft could orbit the earth. American and Russian scientists were now developing rockets that would carry spacecraft farther out into space.

In 1958, the Russians launched rockets that carried spacecraft around the moon. The Americans, in 1960, sent their rockets into orbit. These rockets carried satellites for weather forecasting, communications, and navigation purposes.

No one had yet put an astronaut into a spacecraft. It was clear, however, that both Americans and Soviets were working toward this goal.

First into orbit

On April 12, 1961, a rocket took off from the launchpad at Tyuratam in Russia.

It carried a spacecraft, *Vostok 1*, and an astronaut, Yury Gagarin.

The rocket slowly rose from the ground. Its speed increased as it surged upward into the sky. A few minutes later, *Vostok 1* went into orbit around the earth, at an **altitude** of 205 miles (327 km). It made one orbit and landed safely 108 minutes after liftoff. The spacecraft landed using parachutes, but Gagarin himself came down separately, with his own parachute.

Gagarin will always be remembered as the first person to orbit the earth.

"Project Mercury"

Less than a month after Gagarin's flight, an American rocket lifted off from the launch site at Cape Canaveral, Florida. It carried the spacecraft *Freedom 7* and the

▼ Yury Alekseyevich Gagarin, age 27, was a major in the Russian Air Force. He became the world's first astronaut.

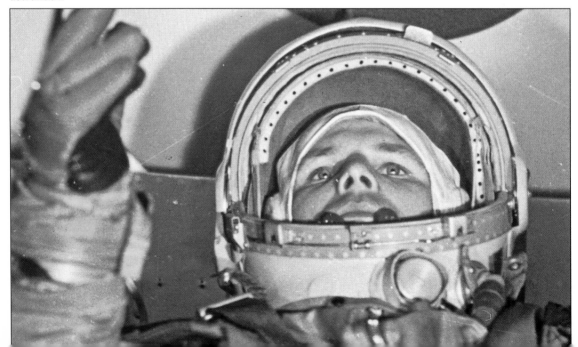

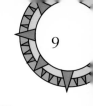

▲ Alan Shepard

first American astronaut, Alan Shepard. It was part of the American space program called Project Mercury.

Freedom 7 reached an altitude of 118 miles (188 km). The flight lasted 15 minutes 22 seconds. This spacecraft did not orbit the earth, but went straight up and back down to earth. The distance from launchpad to **splashdown** in the ocean was only 303 miles (486 km), but the Americans, too, were making progress.

Future plans

On May 25, 1961, President John F. Kennedy announced an important new space program. It was called the Apollo Project. President Kennedy said that within ten years the United States would land an astronaut on the moon. It was only six weeks after Gagarin's historic spaceflight. America had offered a challenge, and the space race had begun!

G forces

Astronauts experience enormous forces when spacecraft change speed quickly. These forces are called **G forces** because they are based upon the force of gravity. Ordinary human activity is carried out at "1G"—the force of gravity on earth. Astronauts, however, are faced with forces of up to 20G, which could crush a human body.

Astronauts are trained to deal with G forces in a machine called a centrifuge. It swings a cage around in a circle. The astronaut is strapped into the cage. The machine speeds up and the forces build up from the center of the circle. They push the astronaut toward the edge of the cage. This centrifugal force makes the astronaut feel heavier, and his or her movements slow down. The machine then twists the cage in different directions. These movements imitate, or **simulate**, what it is like to be in a spacecraft in flight. The astronaut is left feeling dizzy and tired for hours after being in a centrifuge.

▼ *Vostok I* carries Yury Gagarin into space

The Space Race

Early in 1962, the United States was ready to send an astronaut into orbit around the earth. On February 20, the spacecraft *Friendship 7*, powered by an Atlas rocket, lifted off from Cape Canaveral. On board *Friendship 7* was astronaut John Glenn. The spacecraft orbited the earth three times, then successfully splashed down in the Atlantic Ocean. Glenn was given a hero's reception by the American public.

New technology and new skills

Both Americans and Soviets were working toward a moon landing. Before this could happen, more powerful spacecraft had to be developed, and new space skills learned. The most powerful rocket developed by the Americans was the Saturn V, which would be used on moon flights. The Russians also built a more powerful rocket, called the Proton.

The Gemini Project

The next American series of flights was called the Gemini Project. The new spacecraft were bigger and could carry two astronauts instead of one. They could travel farther and stay in orbit longer. The astronauts would be able to control these new craft themselves, instead of relying on control from the scientists at Mission Control in Houston, Texas.

Space walk

A Russian craft, *Voskhod II*, (*voskhod* means "sunrise") was launched on March 18, 1965, with two astronauts on board. As

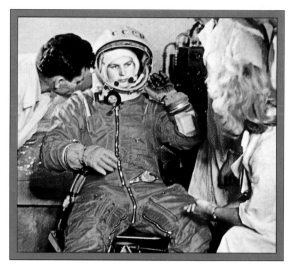

▲ On June 16, 1963, Valentina Tereshkova became the first woman to go into space. She spent almost three days making 48 orbits of the earth in the spacecraft *Vostok 6*, before returning safely. While in space, Tereshkova's craft came within 3 miles (5 km) of another Soviet astronaut, Valery Bykosky. Bykosky's craft, *Vostok 5*, had been launched two days before Tereshkova and *Vostok 6*.

the spacecraft went into its second orbit, one of the astronauts, Alexei Leonov, opened an air hatch and carefully climbed out into space. A thin line attached to his space suit stopped him from floating away from the craft. Leonov floated around outside for a few minutes, while a television camera on the craft sent pictures to earth. After this historic space walk, Leonov returned to the spacecraft, and the two astronauts returned safely to earth.

Docking

In March 1966, the United States launched the spacecraft *Gemini 8*. There were two

▲ In June 1965, American astronaut Ed White spent 15 minutes "walking" in space outside this spacecraft, *Gemini 4*.

astronauts on board—Neil Armstrong, the commander, and Dave Scott. At a separate launch, an *Agena* craft was sent up without astronauts. American scientists wanted to see whether the two spacecraft could meet up in space. Armstrong steered *Gemini 8* for almost five hours to approach *Agena*'s orbit. The two craft came so close that their **hatches** were able to lock together. It was the first successful joining, or **docking**, of two spacecraft.

Space suits

There is no air in space, so an astronaut wears a space suit, which supplies oxygen for breathing. The suit also supplies air pressure to the astronaut's body. Without the correct pressure, the fluids in the astronaut's body would not function properly, and he or she would die.

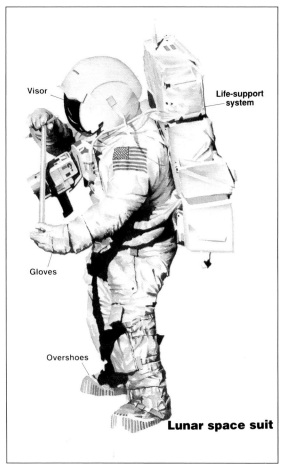

Visor

Life-support system

Gloves

Overshoes

Lunar space suit

Mapping the moon

American and Russian scientists and engineers were building rockets and spacecraft and training astronauts for a moon landing. Yet there were many unanswered questions about the moon itself. What would a spacecraft land on? Was the surface so deep in dust that the craft might sink into it and be lost forever? Was it too rocky to land safely? People knew there was no atmosphere—no air for the astronauts to breathe—but what other dangers were there?

Both countries launched spacecraft called **probes**, to try to find the answers to some of these questions.

Luna

In 1959, the Soviets launched *Luna 1*, which passed within 3,700 miles (6,000 km) of the moon. Nine months later *Luna 2* reached the moon, but crashed on its surface at a speed of 7,500 mph (12,000 kph).

This was followed by a real success. *Luna 3*, equipped with a camera, transmitted back to earth pictures of the far side of the moon. That is the side that is always dark and hidden from the earth.

The Russians were working at ways of controlling the speed of a craft as it neared the moon's surface. In January 1966, the spacecraft *Luna 9* was approaching the moon. As it came nearer to the moon, rockets were fired that faced away from the direction of travel. These **retro-rockets** slowed the speed of the spacecraft. A package of scientific instruments was

released from the craft and landed safely on the moon's surface. It was the first safe —or soft—moon landing. The package opened automatically, and the instruments sent pictures back to earth. They were taken from a height of only 2 feet (0.6 meter), and they provided very good information about the surface of the moon.

Surveyor

A new American probe, *Surveyor 1*, made a soft landing on the moon in June 1966. It sent back thousands of pictures. *Surveyor 1* was powered by batteries that obtained electricity from the sun's rays. This type of battery is called a solar cell.

Surveyor 3 landed on the moon on April 20, 1967. This probe carried a mechanical scoop, which dug trenches into the surface. It tested, or **analyzed**, the surface material. It now seemed certain that a

▼ *Surveyor 3* on the surface of the moon

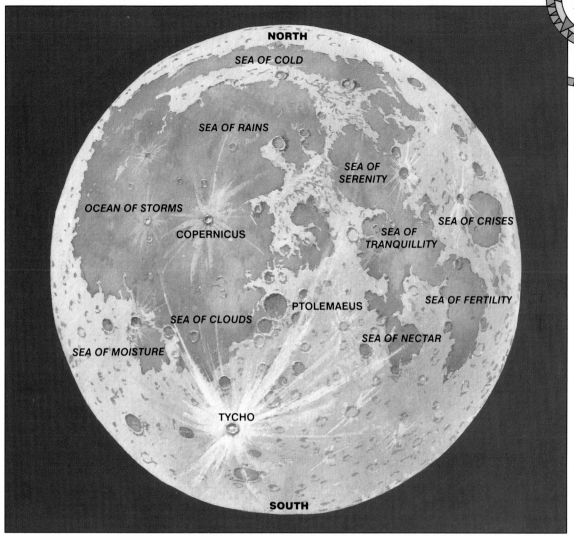

NORTH

SEA OF COLD

SEA OF RAINS

SEA OF
SERENITY

OCEAN OF STORMS

SEA OF CRISES

COPERNICUS

SEA OF
TRANQUILLITY

PTOLEMAEUS

SEA OF FERTILITY

SEA OF CLOUDS

SEA OF NECTAR

SEA OF MOISTURE

TYCHO

SOUTH

▲ Moon "seas" are unlike seas on earth—there is no water on the moon. From the earth, though, there are areas on the moon's surface that looked as though they might be seas. They were given the names of "seas" or "oceans."

▼ Cape Canaveral was renamed Cape Kennedy in 1963 in memory of President John F. Kennedy. In 1973 it was called Cape Canaveral again.

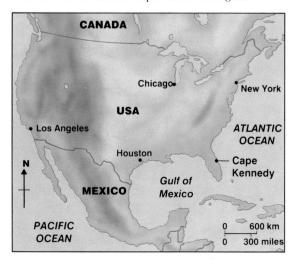

CANADA

Chicago

New York

USA

Los Angeles

ATLANTIC
OCEAN

Houston

Cape
Kennedy

N

MEXICO

Gulf of
Mexico

PACIFIC
OCEAN

0   600 km

0   300 miles

spacecraft could land safely, without sinking into moon dust.

Landing sites

The Americans then turned their attention toward finding a suitable landing place for spacecraft. After the *Surveyor 7* probe in January 1968, they felt that they had all the information they needed. A landing site had been selected. It was to be on the Sea of Tranquillity.

The Apollo Project

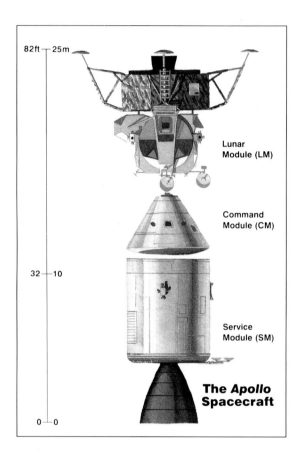

82ft — 25m

Lunar
Module (LM)

Command
Module (CM)

32 — 10

Service
Module (SM)

**The *Apollo*
Spacecraft**

0 — 0

The Apollo Project was the name given to the space program that aimed to land people on the moon. The plan was to use a powerful rocket that would carry the spacecraft and its crew away from the earth. The craft would have its own engines and fuel, and it would be able to separate into two spacecraft. One of these craft, the moon lander, would land on the surface of the moon, while the other stayed in orbit around the moon. Then the moon lander would take off from the moon and dock with the orbiting craft. The astronauts would then return to earth.

The spacecraft

The *Apollo* spacecraft consisted of three main parts. Each part was called a **module**.

The **command module** carried the astronauts and the controls. The **service module** carried the supplies, engines, and fuel for the command module. These two modules were attached together and were called the command service module, or CSM.

The third part of the spacecraft was the moon lander, or **lunar module**. It had its own engines and fuel and could operate as a separate spacecraft.

It was calculated that the total weight of the *Apollo* spacecraft would be about 46 tons. The Americans then needed a rocket that could lift this weight clear of the earth's gravity and push it toward the moon.

Saturn V

A new type of **booster** rocket was developed, called the Saturn V, that had three stages of engines. Each stage would fire in turn, pushing the spacecraft higher and higher into space.

Saturn V was first tested in November 1967, carrying an *Apollo* spacecraft but no astronauts. Two minutes and forty seconds after launch, the first stage shut down on schedule and the second-stage engines fired. Three minutes later, the second stage shut down on schedule and the third-stage engines fired, carrying the CSM into orbit around the earth. Nine hours after launch,

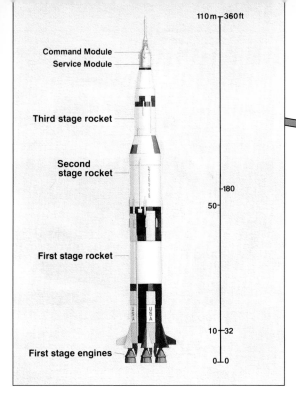

Command Module
Service Module

Third stage rocket

Second
stage rocket

First stage rocket

First stage engines

110 m — 360 ft

180

50

10 — 32

0 — 0

▼ The Saturn V rocket stood over 360 feet (110 meters) tall. It weighed more than 3,000 tons and was the world's largest rocket.

the CSM splashed down in the Pacific Ocean. The tests had worked perfectly.

In January 1968, *Apollo 5* successfully tested the engines of the lunar module.

Further training

Meanwhile, the astronauts' training included getting used to new space suits and to spaceflight and its particular problems. This included anything that might go wrong with the spacecraft while out in space. The astronauts trained by using imitation spacecraft called **simulators**, linked up to computers.

The simulators are laid out exactly like the inside of a real spacecraft, with dials and gauges that behave as the real instruments would. The computer makes the simulator act as though something is wrong—for example, an oxygen tank will spring a leak. Then a pressure gauge will start to fall, and the astronaut must fix the problem. The astronauts spent many hours in the simulator, practicing what to do if anything did go wrong.

▼ The crew of the *Apollo 7* flight

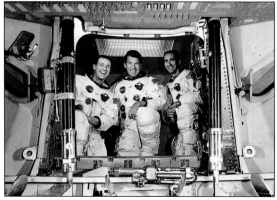

The far side of the moon

The next part, or phase, of the testing involved taking an *Apollo* spacecraft out of earth's orbit, around the moon, and back to earth. Astronauts would be on board, so everything had to work correctly. If anything went seriously wrong, the results could be tragic.

Apollo 8

Apollo 8 consisted of a Saturn V rocket and a command and service module. On board were astronauts Frank Borman (mission commander), Jim Lovell, and Bill Anders.

At 7:51 A.M. on December 21, 1968, the Saturn V rocket lifted off the launchpad. Twelve minutes later it went into orbit around the earth. The craft stayed in orbit while the scientists and engineers at Mission Control in Houston, Texas,

▼ *Apollo 8* circled the moon on Christmas Eve, 1968

▲ The crew of the *Apollo 8* flight

checked that everything was working properly. The go-ahead was then given to leave earth's orbit and head toward the moon. As the third stage was fired to give the extra power, the astronauts were slammed back against their seats. The spacecraft was on its way to the moon.

The third part of the rocket was released, but in the weightlessness of space it did not fall away from the spacecraft. Instead, it seemed to follow it for a while.

The next day the craft was more than 100,000 miles (160,000 km) away from earth, in the silence of space. The television camera on board transmitted pictures back to earth. The astronauts had a good view of the earth—Frank Borman described it as "warm, blue . . . with huge covers of white clouds."

Around the moon

The spacecraft's speed slowed as it moved farther away from the earth. As it neared the moon, it began to speed up again as the moon's gravity pulled it. The craft was now less than 1,000 miles (1,600 km) away from the moon. Borman gave the order to fire the retro-rockets to slow down the spacecraft. The crew were strapped into their seats. They were about to swing around the dark side of the moon. When that happened, they would be out of contact with the earth, because the moon would block the signals between the earth and the spacecraft. It would be 40 minutes before the craft would reappear at the other side of the moon. Then contact could be made again with earth. The astronauts would have to decide themselves when to fire the CSM's engine to put the craft into moon orbit.

Frank Borman gave the order to fire the engine. The spacecraft changed direction. The crew waited tensely. If the engine had been fired at the right time, they would see the sun rise above the edge of the moon. Suddenly, there it was—a dazzling glare above the curve of the edge of the moon. They looked down, and the surface of the moon was only 62 miles (100 km) below them. They were in the moon's orbit.

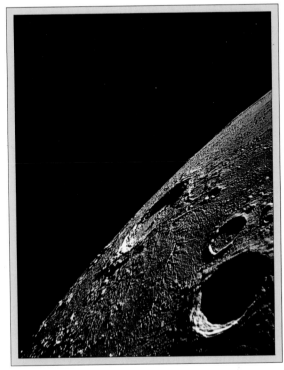

▲ Crater Copernicus on the moon

On earth, the scientists and engineers at Mission Control waited in silence while the CSM was out of contact. Forty minutes later, there was a burst of radio noise, and the transmitters once more received signals from space. *Apollo 8* had traveled around the far side of the moon!

Return

The astronauts spent 20 hours orbiting the moon. On Christmas Day, 1968, *Apollo 8* headed back toward the earth.

The spacecraft splashed down 6 days and 3 hours after its **liftoff** from earth. The **mission** had been a success, and the Americans had completed an important stage in their moon landing program.

Countdown

The Americans carried out two more test flights before they were ready to attempt a moon landing. On March 3, 1969, *Apollo 9* was launched to test the separation and docking procedures of the Lunar and CSM modules. The tests were successful.

Apollo 10

Apollo 10's mission was to test the rocket, the CSM, and the lunar module in orbit around the moon. The go-ahead for the moon landing would be given only if everything worked perfectly on this test flight.

Apollo 10 lifted off on May 18, 1969. Two and a half hours later, the Saturn V rocket fired and pushed the craft out of earth's orbit on course for the moon. Two days later, as *Apollo 10* moved behind the moon, the CSM's engines fired the craft into the moon's orbit. The next day, two of the astronauts climbed into the lunar module. The module separated from the CSM. It descended slowly toward the moon's surface.

The lunar module headed toward the Sea of Tranquillity. This, however, was not to be a moon landing. The module flew to within 47,000 feet (14,460 meters) of the surface, then, 57 minutes after the start of their descent, the astronauts turned the module around and increased engine power. The lunar module rose away from the moon's surface and docked safely with the CSM.

All the tests had been completed successfully. The way was now clear for *Apollo 11* and a moon landing.

Luna 15

Three days before *Apollo 11* was due to lift off, the Russians launched a spacecraft, *Luna 15*. What were their plans? No astronauts were aboard, so it was not an attempt at a moon landing. Might *Luna 15* get in the way of *Apollo 11*'s flight? There was no information from the Russians.

◀ The launch of *Apollo 10*

Frank Borman telephoned the Soviet Academy of Sciences, but was given only the details of *Luna 15*'s moon orbit. Then a Yugoslav news agency reported that *Luna 15*'s mission was to bring moon rock back to earth. Unfortunately, the craft was unable to slow down on its descent to the moon's surface. It crashed and broke up.

Waiting for liftoff

The countryside around Cape Kennedy was packed with people in the early hours of Wednesday, July 16, 1969. More than a million people had gathered to watch the launch of *Apollo 11*. The astronauts, Neil Armstrong, Buzz Aldrin, and Mike Collins, were woken up at 4:15 A.M. They ate a breakfast of steak and eggs. Then they put on the special clothing, space suits, and helmets that they would need for the launch.

The launchpad was deserted. The giant Saturn V rocket stood, loaded with more than 2,000 tons of highly explosive rocket fuel. An elevator took the astronauts up to the top of the rocket, where they were helped into the CSM and strapped into their seats. The hatch was closed. As the sun rose in the sky, the **countdown** began. Sixty seconds before ignition, everything was ready. The countdown continued.

The launch was being shown on television all over the world. Millions of people watched. Everyone knew that this was the historic mission that might put an astronaut on the moon. History was being made before their eyes.

▶ Neil Armstrong was 38 years old, from Ohio. He had been a test pilot before becoming an astronaut. He was the most experienced astronaut on the *Apollo 11* flight, which is why he was chosen as mission commander.

Liftoff

▲ *Apollo 11* lifting off from the launchpad at Cape Kennedy

The astronauts waited as the countdown continued. They glanced at one another and smiled in encouragement. From the firing room could be heard: ". . . five, four, three, two, one, zero, all engines running." There was a rumbling noise. "Liftoff! We have a liftoff." It was 9:32 A.M. The huge rocket went up into the morning sky, burning 15 tons of fuel per second. Mission Control in Houston, Texas, took over control from Cape Kennedy. At a height of 45 miles (72 km), the first stage burned out and fell back toward the ocean. The second-stage engines took over. After nine minutes, the third-stage engine fired. The second stage dropped away. The spacecraft was in orbit around the earth.

Into space

Nearly three hours after liftoff, the third-stage engine was restarted. It moved the spacecraft out of earth's orbit to head toward the moon.

Mike Collins flicked a switch to separate the command service module, called *Columbia*, from the third stage. Then *Columbia* moved forward and flipped itself over completely so that the other end was next to the third stage.

The lunar module, called *Eagle*, was on top of the third stage. *Columbia* docked with *Eagle*, then the third stage was jettisoned. Collins fired *Columbia's* engines. The spacecraft was on its way to the moon.

On board the spacecraft

After five hours in space, the astronauts took off their heavy space suits. They drifted around the craft, choosing comfortable places to settle and rest. They ate their first meal—chicken salad, applesauce, and shrimp cocktail. They tested the television camera on board.

Armstrong looked out of the spacecraft at the earth and told Houston about the weather that was heading toward Central and South America! Collins held the camera while Aldrin took the TV audience on a tour of the spacecraft. After this, the astronauts got into their sleeping bags. There were no beds on the spacecraft, but because the astronauts were weightless, they could rest anywhere.

Nearly 27 hours after liftoff, Collins fired *Columbia's* engines to adjust the spacecraft's course. Everything was going

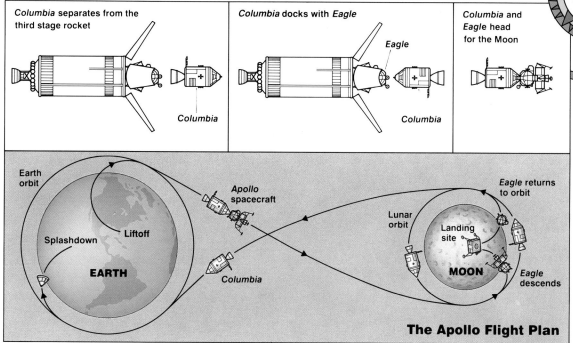

Columbia separates from the third stage rocket

Columbia

Columbia docks with Eagle

Eagle

Columbia

Columbia and Eagle head for the Moon

Earth orbit

Splashdown

Liftoff

EARTH

Apollo spacecraft

Columbia

Lunar orbit

Landing site

MOON

Eagle returns to orbit

Eagle descends

The Apollo Flight Plan

perfectly. They were now halfway to the moon.

Around the moon

Two days later, the spacecraft was ready to swing around behind the moon. The astronauts strapped themselves into their seats. The engine burned for six minutes and *Columbia* went successfully into orbit around the moon.

"The *Eagle* has wings"

Armstrong and Aldrin moved into *Eagle* to prepare for separation from *Columbia*. By the time everything was ready, the spacecraft had orbited the moon twelve times. Collins backed *Columbia* away from *Eagle* and the two craft separated. Armstrong called out, "The *Eagle* has wings."

Houston said that *Eagle* could begin to descend. The descent engine was fired and *Eagle* moved down to a position 8 miles (13 km) above the surface of the moon. Because there were no problems, Houston

gave the astronauts permission to go all the way down to the surface. Armstrong and Aldrin glanced at each other excitedly. This was it. They were going to land on the moon.

▼ Mike Collins was a pilot with the U.S. Air Force. His first experiences as an astronaut were on the *Gemini 10* mission.

Moon landing!

As *Eagle* continued to descend toward the Sea of Tranquillity, under the control of its onboard computer, Armstrong looked out of the window down to the gray, barren surface of the moon. He saw to his alarm that the computer was about to land *Eagle* on rocky, uneven ground.

Armstrong took over control from the computer. He slowed the speed of descent to three feet per second and shifted *Eagle* sideways to a new location. *Eagle* was now only 300 feet (100 m) above the moon's surface, but the ground was still too rocky for a safe landing. As Aldrin called out the figures of height and horizontal speed, Armstrong moved *Eagle* away from the rocks. At a height of 200 feet (65 m), he slowed again. There was another problem now—they were almost out of fuel. (There was plenty of fuel for *Eagle* to take off

▼ *Eagle* on the moon's surface

again, but this was in a separate fuel tank.) Armstrong searched for a smooth landing site. *Eagle* dropped farther. Aldrin called out the figures. Thirty feet (9 meters) to go. There was only a few seconds of descent fuel left. Aldrin watched the shadow of one of *Eagle*'s feet touch the surface. *Eagle* rocked slightly and steadied. Armstrong switched off the engine. Armstrong and Aldrin shook hands. The message was sent to Houston—"Tranquillity Base here. The *Eagle* has landed."

Moon walk

Armstrong and Aldrin spent several hours preparing to leave *Eagle*. They put on big backpacks containing oxygen, water, electrical power, and radio equipment. These backpacks were their **life-support units**. Without them, the astronauts could not survive on the surface of the moon.

Seven hours after landing, Armstrong opened the hatch. He backed out of *Eagle*, moving slowly. His feet found the ladder leading down to the ground and he started climbing slowly down the ladder. He reached over and set up a TV camera on the outside of *Eagle*. He stepped forward and put his foot directly onto the powdery gray surface and said, "That's one small step for a man, one giant leap for mankind."

Aldrin joined Armstrong on the moon's surface. They walked, or rather, bounced, because of the weaker gravity, into the hot sunlight, enjoying the exercise. One of Aldrin's tests was to jog away from *Eagle* to

▲ Edwin Aldrin, Jr., known to his friends as "Buzz," was 39 years old and a colonel in the U.S. Air Force.

see if he could stop and turn without falling over. He found it very difficult!

Raising the flag

Armstrong unveiled a plaque he had set up beside *Eagle*. The plaque read:

HERE MEN FROM THE PLANET EARTH FIRST SET FOOT UPON THE MOON JULY 1969 A.D. WE CAME IN PEACE FOR ALL MANKIND

While Armstrong collected 40 pounds (18 kg) of rocks to take back to earth, Aldrin took the United States flag from *Eagle* and pushed it into the ground. Because there was no wind on the moon, the flag was held out straight by a piece of wire. Then the astronauts spoke to President Richard M. Nixon. He told them, "For one priceless moment, in the whole history of man, all the people on this earth are truly one."

The astronauts left behind a small collection of medals and badges in memory of astronauts who had died in the course of space exploration. Then they climbed back into *Eagle*. The hatch was closed and the astronauts took off their helmets. They had a snack of cocktail sausages and fruit punch and settled down for a well-earned sleep.

Leaving the moon

Seven hours later, Armstrong and Aldrin prepared to leave the moon. After all the flight checks had been completed, Houston gave *Eagle* permission to liftoff. Aldrin counted down, ". . . four, three, two, one. . . proceed." The liftoff was powerful. *Eagle* rose swiftly—somewhere up there, *Columbia* was waiting to meet them.

▼ Armstrong and Aldrin were the first people to see the earth from the surface of the moon.

Return to earth

Four hours after liftoff from the Sea of Tranquillity, *Eagle* docked successfully with *Columbia*. Collins opened the link tunnel between the two spacecraft, and Armstrong and Aldrin made their way back into *Columbia*. They brought with them the boxes of moon rocks and soil that they had collected from the moon's surface.

Collins released *Eagle* from *Columbia*, and the lunar module was left to orbit around the moon. The astronauts then increased *Columbia*'s speed by 2,000 mph (3,200 kph)—enough to push the craft out of the moon's orbit. *Columbia* swung out from behind the moon for the last time, on course for earth. The astronauts were on their way home.

Reentry

Throughout the return journey to earth, *Columbia* and Houston stayed in communication. The journey passed without incident. The Command Module and the Service Module separated successfully. The Command Module then reentered earth's atmosphere safely and splashed down in the Pacific Ocean on July 24, 1969. The astronauts were lifted onto a helicopter and taken to the aircraft carrier USS *Hornet*.

In quarantine

The three astronauts lived in a special trailer on the ship. It was important to keep them away from everyone else on the aircraft carrier. No one knew what germs

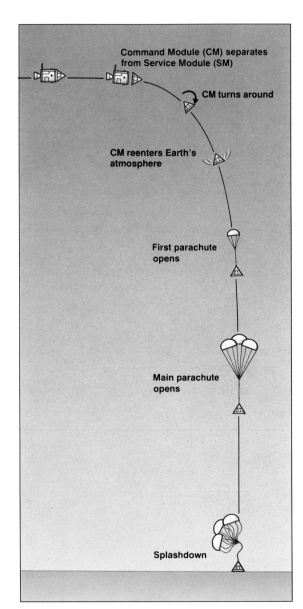

Command Module (CM) separates from Service Module (SM)

CM turns around

CM reenters Earth's atmosphere

First parachute opens

Main parachute opens

Splashdown

▲ Return to earth

or infections they might have brought back from the moon. Being isolated from other people for health reasons is called being in **quarantine**.

In the trailer, the astronauts showered and changed their clothes. Then they were

▲ Splashdown in the Pacific Ocean

told that President Nixon had arrived on the *Hornet* to welcome them back officially. They were only able to appear at the window of the trailer to wave to the television cameras.

The astronauts were transferred from the aircraft carrier—still in the trailer—to Houston. After twenty days, they were found to be in excellent health and their quarantine was ended.

▼ The successful astronauts

Triumphant return

On August 13, 1969, the successful astronauts went on a triumphant tour of New York, Chicago, and Los Angeles. In New York they rode in an open car along Broadway, in front of thousands of cheering people. The air was full of pieces of paper called **ticker tape**, which had been thrown down from the tall office buildings.

Armstrong, Aldrin, and Collins also appeared before Congress and went on a trip around the world. They visited 25 countries in 38 days. Everywhere the astronauts were greeted by joyful crowds. They were given honorary membership in all sorts of organizations. There was even one called the Camel Drivers' Radio Club of Kabul, in Afghanistan. A strange honor for an astronaut!

Later moon shots

▲ *Apollo 15* splashes down in the Pacific Ocean

Following the success of *Apollo 11*, a further six *Apollo* missions were sent out, five of which landed on the moon and returned safely.

Apollo 12 lifted off on November 14, 1969, and shortly afterward was struck by lightning. Luckily, no damage was done and the mission continued as planned. This time the lunar module was guided more accurately toward the landing site —it landed just 585 feet (180 meters) away from the unmanned *Surveyor 3* probe, which had landed there two and a half years earlier. The astronauts were even able to bring parts of the probe back to earth.

Apollo 13

The rocket for the *Apollo 13* mission was launched from Cape Kennedy on April 11, 1970. Fifty-six hours later, as the spacecraft was 206,250 miles (330,000 km) from earth, astronaut Jack Swigert called Houston, "Hey, we've got a problem here." There had been an explosion in an oxygen tank in the command service module. It had severely damaged the service module and stopped the power supply to the command module. There was now no question of landing on the moon.

The problem was how to bring the astronauts back safely to earth. The lunar module's power supply was separate from that of the CSM, so its engine was used to

▲ The Lunar Roving Vehicle on the moon

▲ An astronaut examines a moon boulder

swing the craft around the moon and back toward the earth. Just before reentry, the lunar module was jettisoned and the damaged service module was detached, too. The astronauts reentered the earth's atmosphere in the command module, which splashed down faultlessly. What could have been a tragedy turned out to be a triumph.

Lunar Roving Vehicle

Apollo missions 14 through 17 all made successful moon landings. Each mission explored tougher and rockier ground, and the astronauts spent more time out of the lunar module. They brought back more and more moon rocks. Missions 15, 16, and 17 also took with them the **Lunar Roving Vehicle** to help the astronauts to travel on the moon. This was a lightweight battery-powered vehicle that could be driven at a top speed of 10.5 mph (17 kph). However, it never actually traveled more than 6 miles (9 km) away from the lunar module because the astronauts would have had to walk back to the spacecraft if the vehicle had broken down.

The last manned flight to the moon was *Apollo 17*, in December 1972. The astronauts spent 22 hours outside the lunar module on the surface of the moon. They brought back 246 pounds (112 kg) of rocks.

The future

As a result of the Apollo Project and the Russians' unmanned probes, we now know much more about the moon. We know about its surface, its age, and its internal structure. The moon rocks are similar to rocks on earth, but the oldest moon rocks are about a billion years older than the earth—about 4.5 billion years old.

Scientists have now turned their attention toward other planets and toward developing new methods of space travel.

Space stations

On April 19, 1971, the Soviets launched a huge Proton rocket into earth orbit. On board was a space station, *Salyut 1*. It was 52 ft (16 m) long, weighed 19 tons, and was the world's first scientific **laboratory** in space.

A *Soyuz 11* rocket, carrying three Russian astronauts, docked with *Salyut 1* on June 7, 1971. The astronauts opened the hatches between the two spacecraft and went through to the space station. There they "set up home," and then carried out scientific experiments and made observations of space. They made TV broadcasts to the people in Russia showing themselves at work. The astronauts stayed in *Salyut 1* for 23 days. Unfortunately, they died in an accident on their way back to earth. The orbiting laboratory broke up in October 1971. The Russians later built larger space stations. By 1982, two astronauts were able to spend nearly seven months on *Salyut 7*.

▼ Astronauts training at Houston, Texas

▲ *Skylab* in orbit above the earth

Skylab

American space technicians had also been developing a permanent space station. This was known as *Skylab* and was launched by a Saturn V rocket into earth orbit on May 14, 1973. *Skylab* had an overall length of 117 ft (36 m) and weighed over 90 tons.

Skylab was a fully equipped laboratory, with sleeping space for the crew. The comforts for the crew included a zero-gravity shower for washing, and exercise machines to keep the astronauts fit. The astronauts on board *Skylab* carried out observations of the sun and stars and the earth. They also made various experiments. One of these was to find out if a spider could still spin its web in zero gravity. The spider was confused at first, but soon it started spinning happily! In another experiment they grew crystals in zero gravity. These crystals were bigger and better than those grown on earth. The astronauts also studied the effects of weightlessness upon human beings.

Skylab stayed in orbit long after the

▲ Space shuttle *Endeavour* lifts off

astronauts stopped visiting it. In July 1979, however, it reentered earth's atmosphere and broke up.

Space shuttle

American scientists decided to try to build a spacecraft that could be used more than once. This led to the development of the space shuttle. The shuttle was more like an airplane than a command service module.

The first launch of the space shuttle *Columbia* took place on April 12, 1981, from Cape Canaveral. The shuttle went into orbit on a two-day mission and then landed at Edwards Air Force Base in California. It landed like an airplane, not like a spacecraft. Its real success came seven months later, when it landed after its second mission in space. For the first time in history, a spacecraft had made more than one flight in space. The time of the reusable spacecraft had arrived. The space shuttle was used to take crews into orbit for scientific experiments and to put communications satellites into orbit.

Other planets

Along with these successes, American and Russian space scientists have also launched probes toward other planets. One day soon, astronauts may be sent to Mars or even Venus.

Moon base?

In the future, it is likely that the materials used to build large space stations will come from the moon, rather than being sent from earth. These space stations will be used as bases for sending astronauts to other, more distant planets. It is also likely that permanent bases will be set up on the moon for scientific observations of the stars and earth. The moon, our nearest neighbor, may become very important to us in the future. It will probably not be long before other people arrive there, following in the footsteps of the three astronauts who led the way.

▼ The space shuttle landing in 1992

Glossary

air pressure:	the force of gravity that holds the layer of atmosphere around the earth
altitude:	height, usually above the level of the sea
analyze:	to examine in detail
astronaut:	a traveler in space (the name comes from Latin words that mean "star sailor")
atmosphere:	the air around the earth
booster:	something that gives a short burst of extra power
command module:	the part of the *Apollo* spacecraft that contained the astronauts and the controls
countdown:	as the time before an event gets shorter, it is "counted down"
docking:	the joining of two spacecraft
G force:	a measure of the force of gravity
gravity:	the force that pulls objects down to earth or another body in space
hatch:	a flat opening in a spacecraft
laboratory:	a place for carrying out scientific tests
launchpad:	the site where space rockets take off
life-support unit:	a small pack carried on an astronaut's back when outside the spacecraft
liftoff:	when a rocket leaves the ground
lunar module:	the part of the *Apollo* spacecraft that would land on the moon
Lunar Roving Vehicle:	a vehicle that was specially adapted for use on the moon
mission:	a task that a person, or a group of people, set out to achieve
module:	a separate part of a spacecraft
orbit:	a path taken by something when it circles an object
oxygen:	a gas that people need to breathe in order to stay alive
planet:	a large object in space that goes around a sun
probe:	a small spacecraft that doesn't carry astronauts. Probes usually test conditions before astronauts' lives are risked.

quarantine: in isolation, for health reasons

retro-rocket: a rocket fired to slow speed down, rather than to increase it

satellite: a small object in space that circles a planet or a moon

service module: the part of the *Apollo* spacecraft that contained the supplies, engines, and fuel

simulate: to imitate real conditions

simulator: something that imitates real conditions. It allows people to practice reacting to dangers.

spacecraft: a vehicle for traveling in space

space suit: an astronaut's clothing

splashdown: to land in the sea after a spaceflight

ticker tape: thin strips of paper on which messages were coded in patterns of holes. It was an American city tradition to shower pieces of this tape onto people in a parade through the streets below the office windows.

Further Reading

Apfel, Necia. *Space Station*. New York: Franklin Watts, 1987.

Coric, Charles P., ed. *Space Exploration: Opposing Viewpoints*. San Diego: Greenhaven Press, 1992.

Cross, Wilbur. *Space Shuttle* (revised edition). Chicago: Childrens Press, 1987.

Sullivan, George. *The Day We Walked on the Moon: A Photo History of Space Exploration*. New York: Scholastic, 1990.

Vbrova, Zuza. *Space and Astronomy*. New York: Gloucester Press, 1989.

Williams, Brian. *Twenty Names in Space Exploration*. North Bellmore, New York: Marshall Cavendish, 1990.

Index